MOTIVATION AND KNOWLEDGE

MOTIVATION AND KNOWLEDGE

Dr. Roham Ghassemi

Library of Congress Control Number: 2022921231
ISBN: Hardcover   978-1-6698-5589-7
                     Softcover   978-1-6698-5588-0
                     eBook   978-1-6698-5587-3

Print information available on the last page.

Rev. date: 11/11/2022

To order additional copies of this book, contact:
Xlibris
844-714-8691
www.Xlibris.com
Orders@Xlibris.com
847600

For years, my heart was looking for the water of life.
It was seeking something that he already contained.

—Divan Hafez, page 127

MANY PERSONAL AND social problems and conflicts would perhaps be resolved before turning into issues if we would use words on condition of knowing their meanings, rather than just knowing or recognizing the word because of hearing it over and over again. That's always true in our everyday life, starting within ourselves or with communication with others.

For example, we think of a word like motivation, and we start to think about it and then want to take action. But we truly don't know the meaning of motivation, so we think it must be some sort of energy or power or fuel to get us to be more active toward our goals. We think it's something that we are missing and we take action to have it, yet we truly don't know what it means. Then after a few minutes or hours or days, we give up. We don't feel the motivation any more, or we forget the feeling of motivation as it was originally, and we don't see much value in it. Then the negative thinking of not being capable starts, and after, the feeling of sadness sets in.

We experience that in communicating with others as well. When we explain a subject to someone, and before we complete the sentence, they make the rational saying, "I know what you mean," without having had the same experience of joy, pain, victory, etc. They just say, "I know, I know," and after explaining more and more, they admit they haven't had the same experience as you have. We experience this type of assumption about knowledge and knowing every day without realizing we do it. This pattern of thinking and behavior is what needs to be corrected for the individual to be able to have a more realistic thinking and approach to setting goals and moving forward with them.

In cognitive behavior therapy today, the cognitive model proposes that dysfunctional thinking is common to all psychological disturbances. When people learn to evaluate their thinking in a more realistic and adoptive way, they experience a decrease in negative emotion and maladaptive behavior (*Cognitive Behavioral Therapy: Basics and Beyond,* J. S. Beck, page 4). To be thinking in a more realistic and adoptive way is the way we start to learn about ourselves, which has to do with "Why would I? What would I? How would I?" and many other questions that stop us from being motivated. Therefore, this type of thinking helps with our level of cognition and knowledge about ourselves. CBT has had many successes in different areas of psychology because of this very reason that it bases treatment on a cognitive formulation.

Paying attention to realistic thinking and cognition at different levels of all the research that many have done and presented to us would help with gathering information step by step for true knowledge. That is why I am about to explain the importance of knowledge here by carefully paying attention to what the wise have said about true knowledge instead of just knowing information about knowledge or motivation.

To get a better idea of the base of our search, I like to refer to and review some of the works of great philosophers and the wise throughout history to the present. We come closer to the real meaning behind words we use, such as motivation, and to realize a real, comprehensible picture of knowledge of self, and realizing the importance of having motivation is in line with knowing the self or self-cognition. Then we will pay more attention to the levels of knowledge or cognition of the self.

What I'm sharing here is based on my personal research and experience on the subject of motivation and knowledge, which would not have had any meaning or value without the practical guidance that I've had. Prof. Nader Angha uses an important base for seeking knowledge. He says, "Know yourself first to know your necessities." That means, everything we do and learn has to do with knowledge, which has to do with knowing yourself; otherwise, there is no true value to that knowledge.

One of the most common issues among people, especially youth, is struggling with lack of motivation. This could be lack of motivation for studying, exercising, working, or even motivation for waking up early and starting the day to just be cheerful. Being unmotivated is considered so normal that it is customary and often discussed as if it is a new trend, a new mystery topic to ramble or complain about, and to which there is no practical and correct answer. Take the instance of a friend of yours from college that you meet on the street after a few days of absence from their classes. When asked about the reason why he has been missing school, he first shrugs the matter aside, saying, "I am busy with some personal matters." And then when you curiously ask about the details, he may finally say he "has lost motivation for studying" and that's why he is not attending his classes and trying to figure what he wants to do with life and his future.

Treating lack of motivation as a scapegoat or an excuse or merely something to chat about seems to be spreading like a disease among people of different ages. Sadly, many have lost motivation themselves, and because of that, they feel helpless and find it hard to help others. But since they are unaware of their loss and the value of what is lost, they do not seem to be searching for it, especially when they don't see or hear a solution for it or anyone to guide them in the right satisfactory direction. The answer may exist within us if we really want to know it from within. Being too busy listening to scattered information that surrounds us internally as well as externally, we completely ignore it and don't bother with it.

Prof. Nader Angha said, "Human beings are part of existence, and as such, they are in harmony with it. However, outside limitations imposed on them prevent them from realizing this harmony" (*Theory "I"* 2002). When the baby is in his mother's womb, it is part of the mother's body, and it is in complete harmony with the existence of where it exists. As soon as it is born and starts experiencing the outside limitations and interactions, it slowly becomes distant from that harmony.

As a child, the main goal toward growing and self-actualization is to have needs met and to be cared for, to be taught and to be trained to implement the teachings and grow year after year, then go to school and learn to be trained. If this process is uninterrupted, the child will have the motivation to continue to learn and grow. Being motivated to excel, we have to agree there are always outside factors and limitations from the environment that may play a role in encouragement and discouragement of the child's motivation.

That plus other factors, such as freedom and knowledge, which contribute to having motivation, is the subject of our discussion here.

I have been taught for many years: In order to learn, you need to know you don't know and then seek to know. After you learn, like any concerned and responsible individual, you should do your best to help others to know through practical and professional means and not be clouded by personal attributes, feelings, and motives.

In my substance abuse treatment thesis, I shared my research in examining the current work on substance abuse treatments with cognitive behavioral therapy and self-efficacy theory, self-evaluation, and self-cognition strategies to identify components of the above that are empirically important and might logically be included in a substance abuse treatment program. Through a critical analysis of existing theory related to CBT and self-efficacy, the components that might be included in an intervention to reduce substance use were identified.

In my thesis, self-efficacy and self-evaluation are just two types of components of self-cognition, which I was able to explain how it could motivate a person to have a better self-confidence and self-esteem to deal with staying away from desires they could not control. When we look in any field of psychology, we can realize the true self-cognition must have more components that needs to be explained, which also points us to different levels of self-knowledge, to help with motivation.

After noticing the lack of motivation among people at different ages and different levels, I paid close attention to this widespread issue, as I experienced the same problem when I was younger and needed guidance. I began to realize the critical importance of it, so I started to carefully study its cultural, psychological, and philosophical roots to be able to find and discuss a few comprehensive and practical suggestions.

I would like to humbly ask scholars, teachers, professors, and experts to ignore potential editorial errors in this text and focus on the message itself, and if you find any part in this that needs more explanation, you can try to shed your own light upon it, so this critical issue be more clearly understood by everyone.

To better organize the text for the reader, I have written a summary of the subjects to be discussed in respective order so that it can serve as an outline, foretelling the reader what to expect.

In the first chapter, we will start to talk about motivation from different perspectives. For example, Carl Rogers (1902–1987) is one of the most influential psychologist in American history. His contributions are outstanding in the fields of education, counseling, psychotherapy, peace, and conflict resolution. In self-actualization, Rogers believes humans are born with a desire to do the best they can and be the best they can. Self-actualization is the motivating force to achieving their full potential.

In the second chapter, we will talk about motivation and its relationship with needs. Maslow explained in great detail the relationship between human needs and motivation through a series of articles named "A Theory of Human Motivation" published in 1943. Through a better understanding of needs and the aforementioned relationship with motivation, one can be better motivated to find a healthy way of to live

The third chapter is about providing perspectives regarding motivation and factors to help being motivated, which is only possible through an awareness and information from different views, and realize, when talking about motivation, how important it is to know about it and find ways within us to relate to it and find the way to be motivated, which is healthy for me, for the *I*.

In the fourth chapter, we will talk about motivations, knowing the obstacles and overcoming them. Prof. Nader Angha says, "Just as precious diamonds do not deteriorate in the dirt of swamps, the veins of pure gold keep their luster within the heart of the earth and are loath to mix with the brittle soil. Human beings also bear a distinctive attribute in their earthly, natural existence, which is luminous and has a life of its own" (*Theory "I"*).

The fifth chapter will be providing the reader with practical tasks designed to noticeably change one's pattern of life and, by repeating and practicing, become motivated to know more about motivation.

CHAPTER ONE

What is motivation?

WE START WITH Johnmarshall Reeve, who said motivation is an internal process. Whether we define it as a drive or a need, motivation is a condition inside us that desires a change, either in ourselves or the environment. When we tap into this well of energy, motivation endows the person with the drive and direction needed to engage with the environment in an adoptive, open-ended, and problem-solving sort of way (Reeve 2015, *Understanding Motivation and Emotion* 6th edition).

Then the basic information about motivation, as Wikimedia explains, is

> motivation is the driving force that causes the flux from desire to will in life. For example, hunger is a motivation that elicits a desire to eat. Motivation has been shown to have roots in physiological, behavioral, cognitive, and social areas. Motivation may be rooted in a basic impulse to optimize well being, minimize physical pain and maximize pleasure. It can also originate from specific physical needs such as eating, sleeping or resting. Motivation is an inner drive to behave or act in a certain manner. These inner conditions such as wishes, desires and goals, activate to move in a particular direction in behavior.

By these explanations, we realize motivation has a direct relation with ourselves and the energy to engage with our environment, which is probably one of the most important factors for our behavior in life. Prof. Nader Angha has said, "First know who you are to know your necessities." Therefore, knowing who I am and what I am doing in this world has to be a condition to knowing motivation.

Motivation has been defined in *Merriam-Webster's Dictionary* as being "a force or influence that causes someone to do something." Since we usually lack a concrete knowledge of the meaning behind the words we use, we repeatedly misuse the word *motivation* and lack a way to control where this drive may take us. This is why we sometimes find ourselves motivated, and at other times, not so.

Having these points in mind, we can see the need to clarify more about the meaning of motivation to the best of our abilities and explore different aspects of it so we can better utilize its drive.

Carl Rogers, a world-famous contemporary psychologist, points out,

> all behavior is motivated by self-actualizing tendencies,
> which drives a person to achieve at his/her highest level.
> As a result of these interactions with the environment
> and others, an individual forms a structure of the self-
> organized, fluid, conceptual pattern of concepts and
> values related to the self.

Carl Rogers was a highly influential humanistic psychologist who developed a personality theory that emphasized the importance of self-actualizing tendency in shaping human personalities. Rogers believed that humans are constantly reacting with their subjective reality

          DR. ROHAM GHASSEMI

(phenomenal field), which changes continuously. Over time, a person develops a self-concept based on all the feedback from this field of reality.

In the development of self-concept, positive regard is key. Unconditional positive regard is an environment that is rid of preconceived notions of value. Conditional positive regard is an environment that is full of conditions of worth that must be achieved to be considered successful. Human beings develop an ideal self and a real self based on the conditional status of positive regard. The difference between the ideal self and the real self is called congruity. Fully functioning people can achieve the good life in which they constantly aim to fulfill their potential and allow their personalities to emanate from their experiences.

He believed that the main reason behind living is the human being's desire to improve. He points out that people are constantly striving to live a better life according to their needs; the same motivation drives one toward growing and achieving. Sigmund Freud, who is inarguably one of the most influential figures of modern psychology, however, believed that people were motivated and limited by anger and libido. One may notice Freud's view of humans will or drive is mainly libido, but it is mainly seen to have a negative effect on behavior.

It is well worth mentioning that such drives—namely, libido and anger— are inefficient in helping one maintain a healthy social and domestic life and can, in fact, lead one toward arrogance, self-centeredness, and selfishness. Such a person will eventually come to lead an imbalanced, isolated, and unhealthy life that is far from a civilized human being who needs to have a balanced life to be healthy mentally and physically.

Before the concept of motivation gets too complicated here, let us concentrate with a simpler example: Every baby, from the moment life begins, lives with the first instinct of having milk, motivation, and desire, without any need for reason and logic. Why is that? The child wants to learn about life and to live, then he wants to move, talk, and experience everything, and he does all this without a moment of pause for as long as there is energy. Is it possible to take away this drive to be alive from the child? Did the child have to learn it, or was it just within him? The child only knew that one behavior and nothing else. So is it possible to take this drive away from the child?

As you might have guessed, the answer is yes. This happens to neglected children, or due to intentional abuse, reproach, and suppression of the child's needs, or unintentionally doing so out of ignorance, which, in either case, could have happened to some unmotivated people in their childhood.

As Mahmoud Sheikh, PhD, points out, motivation is the way human beings see their own world, which provides the impetus required to take action in order to fulfill their needs. Motivation, thus, is inseparable from us since we never stop trying to fulfill our needs. The consequences of this endeavor could either be beneficial or harmful, so the driving force behind it, which is motivation, can be thought of as positive or negative.

Anything and everything one does is to bring them inner satisfaction. Be it an hour of playing a video game or spending time with one's spouse and children, it is to satisfy the self. Since all that one does is driven by a motivation of some sort, knowing the nature of different motivations and the causes behind them can help one act on ones that will bring satisfaction for both ourselves and others. Simply put, any action that will result in fulfillment of one's needs and a sense of physical and/or mental satisfaction can create motivation to do it, and ignoring which would bring anxiety and stress.

It is quite clear that every action is done at a cost and will in return help one gain something. When the loss is lower than the gain, the action is useful, and when it is the other way around, it is harmful. A balanced diet, for instance, helps one to maintain physical health and confidence, while an imbalanced one can cause problems, such as obesity, blood pressure, high cholesterol, low self-esteem, and depression.

The important point to consider is, the benefits of an action can sometimes seem to outweigh its cost at first glance, and the potential damage may not be apparent either. Think of a person who indulges regularly in alcohol and drugs consumption as a hobby and gains a relative and short-lived sense of peace and joy, but will come to pay a great price over time, as they may become addicted and risk everything they hold dear. Because of a negative outcome, the driving motivation had been negative. The exact opposite can also be the case. For example, upon visiting our physician for hypertension, we are presented with two options, which are

1. taking medications regularly forever, and
2. leading a healthier life in terms of diet and exercise.

At first, it might seem like the easier choice is to take a few tablets a day instead of running for thirty minutes and going on a diet, since the second and healthier choice does not seem to offer any immediate benefits, and taking tablets seems like simple and easy price to pay for a cure. So one may not always be motivated to pursue something beneficial because the benefits can sometimes be less immediately in reach. It all depends on my level of knowledge. The less I know about myself and my need, the more I go after easy choices where the true benefit is always less possible.

The word *motivation* is generally used to refer to something resulting in beneficial actions and behaviors, but it happens so often that one is tempted to pursue harmful and easy choices with a short-lived gain because of shortsightedness and clouded judgment. To better understand emotional spontaneous choices, think of the Freudian motivations of desire and anger. It is well worth mentioning that first, what we mean by desire is an umbrella term, including all human emotions, wants, and instincts, which are inherently essential parts of our humanity and can only be thought of as negative motivators when out of balance. Like the behavior or the actions of a person under stress, instead of behaving and talking ordinarily, he acts out of balance.

Sometimes the actions motivated by a positive beneficial motivation may not be as enjoyable as we would like; however, our understanding and knowledge of the matter drives us to pursue it regardless because we know of the benefits in different levels of ourselves and are satisfied with it. Routine exercise would perhaps be a good example, as it might seem like a colossally difficult task, especially for people not accustomed to following routines. However, if one gains a real understanding of the long-term benefits of regular exercise, such as higher self-esteem and physical health, the temporary hardships will not stop one from taking action, even if there are no apparent instant benefits to be enjoyed.

When there are both negative and positive motivations within one, how can they be distinguished from one another? And how can we reduce the negative and increase the positive? This can be achieved by discovering the source of different motivations. Motivation is directly related to

DR. ROHAM GHASSEMI

one's level of knowledge and understanding. The more one's sum of information (or knowledge) is organized, deep, educated, and rational, the more aware they are. On the contrary, disorganized, uneducated, and emotion-clouded knowledge makes up a shallow and inadequate understanding. One's knowledge and cognition determine their worldview and mindset of the world around them and, thus, motivate them to pursue certain goals. Motivation is born out of understanding and awareness, so if one seeks to change their motivations from negative, harmful, and futile to positive, beneficial, and fruitful, one will need to improve their knowledge, as it is one's knowledge that helps one evaluate gain and loss resulting from actions.

Another point to consider is, motivation should spring from within you. Nobody else can force it on you or convey it to you. All one can do for another is to help them better understand their wants and capabilities so they can motivate themselves to pursue fulfillment. Unless one is willing to motivate oneself, neither encouragement nor threats from the outside can drive them to act. It is you who, through your own self-awareness and self-cognition, evaluate and calculate your choices and consequences based on knowledge, will have motivation from within.

Prof. Nader Angha said, "First know who you are to know what your necessities are." Humans consist of different levels of existence from the most surface level in life to the deeper levels of being described by psychologists, scientists, or philosophers. When we talk about self-actualization, we have to ask on what level of self-cognition we are focusing on. Is it just our conscious and unconscious levels? If it's only on the most surface and materialistic level, it may be limited and not vast and complete enough and a helpful description for an individual. As we see motivation for many individuals doesn't last, this may be the reason for loss of motivation when it's not acknowledged and rooted deep enough within an individual. The discoveries and motivations of the wise and great scientists are rooted way deeper within them. Prof. Sadegh Angha says, "The past discoveries are only an introduction to the true scientist and true wisdom is from ones essence" (*Manifestations of Thought*).

Nowadays, research about motivation and ways to improve it is conducted in academic centers to help individuals lead a more fulfilling lives on social, professional, and economical levels. But we still don't see many individuals leading more productive and dynamic domestic lives where their inner potentials are being discovered, free from stress on materialistic levels, and enjoying tranquility and peace from within.

Every person needs to learn and grow and expand in harmony with their own personal abilities. It is only under such circumstances that universities may guide more successful individuals and have more scientific results, just with gaining a better understanding of the real self. By encouraging individual's path of inner knowledge and wisdom, it can bring light to true understanding of the necessities and offer better education to improve lives on different levels.

CHAPTER TWO

ABRAHAM MASLOW DRAWS a direct connection from need to motivation and explains.

Motivation seems to be one of the most important pillars for success in everyone's life and fulfilling one's needs. No one is moved to act unless a need creates the necessity, or the motivation; therefore, understanding one's needs is a key form of awareness that can help one be more motivated. Personal needs can be divided into five intertwined parts, whose fulfillment results in a healthy life as explained in psychology. Many problems emerge when one not only fails to fulfill these needs in correct order, but also lacks complete control over how to fulfill each of them to such an extent that one's endeavors only bring forth disappointment and dissatisfaction. This disappointment, then, clouds one's judgment with a debilitating pessimism, which makes one prefer not to do anything at all. At this point, an individual suffers from being unmotivated.

Let us explore Maslow's hierarchy of needs theory in more detail with slight alterations, considering it is relevant to the topic at hand.

1. Physiological Needs
   Physiological needs are among the most fundamental prerequisites required for life to continue and for other needs

to even begin to matter. These include any and all needs of a person's physical body, including, but not limited to, rest and nourishment through sleeping and eating food. Fulfilling these physiological needs is a vital prerequisite for sustaining any individual's life, and whether consciously and systematic or unconsciously and out of habit and instinct, everyone is constantly striving to satisfy them.

Considering geographical and cultural differences in the traditions of various ethnic groups, the manners in which people seek to fulfill these needs may seem to be different. The more organized, educated, and rich in knowledge a culture is, the richer will be the system they will leave behind for their descendants to follow, regardless of what future generations might decide to do with it. One must also take note that a sophisticated and developed culture cannot, in itself, guarantee healthy fulfillment of its members' needs.

The United States, for instance, is one of the leading countries suffering from an epidemic of obesity and other health problems due to the rise in popularity of fast food products. On the other hand, Mediterranean diet is one of the healthiest and most balanced in the world, according to the British Medical Journal.

At all times, when one is dealing with the fulfillment of one's physiological needs, care should be taken to consider one's physical conditions, such as weight, height, and age. Every individual needs to fulfill their needs to the best of their ability, considering the facilities available.

2. Safety Needs

These include four types of security, which are as follows: housing security, job security, financial security, and personal security. One needs a safe and peaceful haven to rest, eat, and spend time with loved ones in peace; a stable job to sustain oneself financially, which will, in turn, ensure a more sustained domestic life; and, finally, personal safety of one's being so one can have emotional stability and peace. By fulfilling these, one can live without fear and stress, and seek to fulfill the next group of needs.

3. Love and Belonging Needs
    Since humans are emotional beings, they need love and affection, and a sense of belonging to a community or group is a key factor in balancing one's life. Even though the latter may not be a tangible concept for some, one cannot ignore the fact that having a sincere and healthy relationship with one's spouse, family members, friends, and living environment is critical in leading a healthy social life.

    The more mutually sincere such relationships and interactions are, the more satisfied one may feel inside. Therefore, strengthening one's bonds with one's peers is an important need. It is so critical that sometimes, one is overwhelmed to fulfill this need, even when safety and physiological ones are not fulfilled. Through its fulfillment, one feels approved, and approval is a foundation upon which emotional balance and health are established, which are also related to our next topic—esteem.

4. Esteem Needs
    All people live with their needs, and these needs shape one's personality, goals, and behaviors. They create a pillar or core

of inner wisdom, which is an index of one's personal values. In other words, this inner wisdom or real self is what each individual accumulates through experience and education in one's living environment. These needs can be divided into two groups: First is the inner individual needs for awareness and self-esteem to deal with everyday life in society that forms inside of me, and second is the acceptance and approval from outsides for interacting with society and to make sure of succeeding in individual wisdom, which is always ongoing.

These needs were deemed more worthy of more consideration by Alfred Adler and his followers, but were largely treated as trivial by Freudians and psychoanalysts. It is satisfaction, according to one's internal values, which helps maintain self-esteem in individuals, since adhering to them brings a sense of stability and power, which itself is a necessity for a healthy life. Instability, weakness, and helplessness bring forth a miserable life. Therefore, tending to these needs and encouraging individuals to fulfill them is vital for any healthy person in society. Having succeeded in one's daily life and fulfilling one's physiological, safety, and emotional needs will also create a feeling of inner peace and satisfaction, which is, in fact, an important human need.

Balance and stability are achievable through fulfilling any and all of these needs at all individual levels in order, which will also fulfill the need for self-approval and self-cognition. Otherwise, everyone constantly seeks to fulfill them, but since it is mainly done on the surface of each individual, it does not bring self-satisfaction and self-approval on every level and will not result in inner peace.

DR. ROHAM GHASSEMI

5. Self-Actualization Needs

Even fulfilling all the aforementioned needs in correct order
and manners will not result in true peace and satisfaction unless
one manages to fully realize one's potential and capacities. The
musician must make music, the painter must paint, and everyone
must be what they can be. This is called self-actualization.

Kurt Goldstein explored this concept for the first time in an
article. He pointed out that by becoming the best of what one
can be and by fully unlocking one's potential, each individual
can achieve self-actualization. Evidently, this need varies from
person to person, as each individual's abilities and capacities are
different from others. Fulfilling this need requires one to also
strive to satisfy one's other needs as well.

The last need for every human being to fulfill in order to live
in peace, free from feelings of void and weakness, is to know
oneself. To "know thyself," as Plato says in *Republic*, "to know
your true self is the only way that one can live in peace and
tranquility." He believed that only philosophers could live in
a healthy and beautiful way because philosophers constantly
strive to know, and at the heart of this desire is to know oneself.

This knowing of the self is knowing on in every level, knowledge,
strengths, and weaknesses, and soothing and disturbing
thought patterns. In other words, it is knowing one on physical
and spiritual levels. The pursuit of success and balance is only
possible with this knowledge, as one can search for something
only when one knows it—the true meaning of life in full
awareness. Einstein found this in pursuit of physics, Beethoven
in music, and any individual in what they do with love, such as

a gardener or carpenter who works first for the joy of what the craft gives them within and then for external reasons.

The fruit of all these works is perfect in their own kind. A quote usually attributed to Pablo Picasso reads,

> The meaning of life is to find your gift, and the
> purpose of life is to give it away.

Maybe this is why many people have lost the reason, desire, and, finally, motive to live life fully, because they have neither discovered their strengths and talents nor have given themselves a chance to do so. Perhaps one could say they lost the purpose to know, they forgot the need to know who they are, and they don't know themselves.

CHAPTER THREE

Motivation and Knowing a Healthy Life

BERTRAND RUSSEL, IN his book *Power*, says, "The love of power, even though it's one of the most powerful human motivations, it varies among different people, and different motivations limits it, such as love of comfort, love of joy, and sometimes the love of acceptance of others."

Russel points at love of power as the most important motivation; that is, not only for an individual that looks for power to rule, but also for each individual to have power over their true discoveries, their everyday thoughts, feelings, and desires.

The motivation for Carl Rogers' desire to improve for a better life and Maslow's hierarchy of needs theory and the order—we need them. It's all about satisfying our desire to have the power to succeed in what we really want, and we need it to be able to overcome the obstacles of the past, the present, and the unseen. That's why Russel refers to all that desire as love. One's whole self needs to be aware of it and know it and really want it and not give up. Love provides motivation's fuel for the power of knowledge.

As explained, being aware of the purpose of life in general is a requirement for being motivated. So now, we must understand to know—to know ourselves as a whole and not only as what we see in the mirror to benefit from positive motivations. René Descartes says, "Everyone asks themselves these three questions, Who am I? Where do I come from? Where am I going? Some people may only think about these questions once in their life, some maybe for a few hours, and very, very few make it their task in life to find the answer to these questions, and they are the scientists.

When paying attention to the words of these great men, we quickly realize the importance of true knowledge. True knowledge starts from knowing myself, and that's knowing myself on every level, which we will discuss that later in our writings.

René Descartes says, "Some think they can learn and know through hearing a few words what another has learned through twenty years of thinking, while in truth, the sharper and brighter their mind is, the more prone to error and less capable of learning what the truth is."

We can realize the more precious the subject we seek to learn, the more delicate our path is and the easier we can get lost and deviate from the truth.

For instance, when scientists or experts in different fields and disciplines talk of having peace and healthy way to live and how to achieve it, their explanations and definitions are shaped and in alignment by their field of study, whether they are sociologists, psychologist, physicists, or biologists. Even though understanding such explanations and definitions is possible for individuals in the same field, they still don't provide a complete and practical guide for having peace and healthy life.

Even the experts that introduce these fields have a hard time maintaining their own peace and tranquility through the more difficult times of their lives. Some of these issues are based on a more personal level. A part of which may have to do with one's beliefs, and another part of which may have to do with one's culture, regardless of the field of research they are educated in. Prof. Nader Angha points out a very delicate but important factor about studying the work of philosophers or scientists: "When researching about the work of philosophers and scientist, you have to also pay attention to the era they lived in and cultural and political and economical influences as well."

Unfortunately, we often see that many conclusions on personal and cultural levels are drawn without any questioning or validation and are solely based on what is heard or read. These are quickly and blindly integrated into one's beliefs or ideologies. To better illustrate the point, take religion, for instance, or traditional beliefs in different cultures, which are followed without any need for confirming or investigating by each individual for themselves. It is no surprise that the healthy life or peace, which one has been told about, is so far from reach, since it is based on what others have heard and passed onto us without even knowing what it truly means or where it came from themselves.

Einstein says, when one has knowledge of something, one is able to explain it in brief definitions; however, if we ask most people following a religion or tradition, What is peace? they will attempt to define it through long and complex definitions. Is that not the reason why we do not know the meanings of such words as motivation, self, and peace? It is evident that without true knowledge or awareness, one cannot be motivated to live a better life.

Being aware of and knowing what we need is the perfect motivator to help one understand matters clearly and to pursue a healthier life. Knowledge gives one the power to understand one's own needs and to find the healthy life suitable for oneself for the sake of oneself, not because of what one might have been told by others nor by trying to fit in standards set by others. When this power is formed inside one, it is spontaneous and internal. It can drive you and guide you toward a healthier life, toward peace. This is like a newborn baby who is motivated and has desires, from the first day with first breath, to breathe, feel, learn, walk, talk, and finally be alive.

Carl Jung says, "You are what you do, not what you say."

A real motivated person is not after short-term desire. It's always listening to its inner voice, which drives it to the end. The lust is always limited to having short gains, short-term rewards, and then feeling lost again. One must know what he needs to follow it and be steadfast to learn the way and the obstacles on his way to be able to satisfy his inner self, far from getting disappointed or discouraged. The motivated individual will take action and will go forward, just like a baby does as he grows, to finally learn.

Goethe says, "Knowing is not enough, we must apply. Willing is not enough, we must do." So knowing and gathering knowledge is first, and implementing is second, and this needs to continue over and over again.

Goethe says, "It is not enough to take steps, which may someday lead to a goal. Each step must be itself a goal, and a step, likewise." That is why the person that knows itself and knows peace and talks or teaches it must always be at peace. He must always give peace with all he does.

Prof. Nader Angha says, "Sun is the center of light in our solar system. It is light, always gives light. It gives light to everything, everywhere, regardless of what they are."

CHAPTER FOUR

Motivations: Knowing the Obstacles and Overcoming Them

P ROF. NADER ANGHA says, "Just as precious diamonds do not deteriorate in the dirt of swamps, the veins of pure gold keep their luster within the heart of the earth and are loath to mix with the brittle soil. Human beings also bear a distinctive attribute in their earthly, natural existence, which is luminous and has a life of its own" (Theory "I").

Providing and caring too much for children unconditionally is one of the most influential problems among the new generation of parents, which, although springs from parental love, is like an issue befallen families. Parents complain about it at all times, but do not seem to be trying to make any changes. They have even named this phenomenon filiarchy, as though the child has emerged from elsewhere to rule over them, freeing them from responsibility. One must point out that no peach tree can bring forth apricots, or as the saying goes: the apple won't fall far from the tree.

When parents obey every whim of the child from the very beginning or sometimes, even praise, reward, or bribe them against their will to show affection or soothe their anger, it is only logical to assume that they have no acknowledgment of discipline and order, which forms responsibility and commitment toward the life of the child. Such children grow up without learning how to be independent and responsible for their life conditions or to unlock their potential to succeed. In other words, the child grows up to be spoilt and unmotivated. Such parents, unaware of the fact that they raise the child's expectations with every praise and bribe, will come to witness small and then greater problems in the educational and social areas of the child's life.

I spoke to a father of a seventeen-year-old not long ago, who said that his son, being successful at school, asked him a strange and complex question he has been unable to answer yet. His question was "Tell me, Father, if I enter university and get you a bachelor's degree and then continue until I earn a PhD for you, what will my position be in this society?"

The first thing that I asked him was how come his son thought he was studying for your sake and not his own? The first thing that he needs to understand is that knowledge is a must, if one wants to have a good character, especially in today's world, no matter the field, discipline, or profession. Therefore, he must understand that he is studying only and only for his own sake, future, and well-being, not his parents' or anyone else's.

That's what the father has missed to teach and train his son—to know that he, and only he, is responsible for his life today and tomorrow. If he wants a good life, he must work hard to learn and to know he's doing that for himself, not his parents. Yet most of our children are not brought up to understand they go to school to learn and to know—to know who they are and what potentials they have. Instead, they have expectations, and their high expectations will overwhelm them with a sense of helplessness and lack of motivation, which will result in

DR. ROHAM GHASSEMI

failures at school, work, social, and emotional life. Raising the child's expectations will come to a point where not only parents but also the environment will be powerless to satisfy the child. At this point, lack of motivation will begin to reveal itself in the child's educational and professional life and catch parents by surprise.

Even though we are aware of the fact that parents meant well in all they did, what happened to the child was, the parents' unbalanced amount of affection and praise made the child develop an inaccurate sense of self and emotional picture about his actions and self.

One of the reasons is, the praises from parents were offered not to encourage the child's strength, but to glorify his small tasks or accomplishments, as well as mistakes, funny habits, and unhealthy behaviors, which were supposed to be met with discipline and order. The child thought that his wrongs were actually praiseworthy and correct and has now formed what we call a false ideal character. Now this false ideal character is about to enter adulthood and meet life in an environment away from parents. How do you predict this will go? Undoubtedly, far from what he might have had in mind. There will be no sign of the "ideal" he expected, so he will begin to feel weak and helpless against it. Still, the false confidence fed by years of praise from his parents is there and makes him wonder why it cannot help against the real environment. His behaviors will start to tend toward either neurotic or self-isolation.

"A child's true confidence will not shape if he is not encouraged for his real achievements" (Lowen, A. 1983. *Narcissism: Denial of the True Self*).

As mentioned before, the infant wants to discover, experience, see, hear, feel, and simply put, live. His purpose to live drives from his essence, which is the source of motivation. The more orderly and balanced this infant lives and grows, the healthier a person he will become. Then through discovering his abilities, he will be able to be connected internally to his own power and potential. Parents and teachers can guide and educate him as suitable for his age. But what we see in practice is, parents go to one extreme or another. They either care too much and prevent self-discovery in a normal environment or neglect too much and eventually erase this desire and motivation in the child and replace it with shortcomings and parents' personal agendas. Then there are voids and complexes because of neglect. So what happened to the child's self-awareness, self-actualization, and self-discovery? Where is the child's motivation? This want, desire, need, and power is on-hold, waiting. Unless the boundaries and obstacles clear the way, it is powerless. There is no manifestation of motivation. The child's self ceases to exist.

Prof. Nader Angha says, "The eternal dimension lies hidden within human beings and is inaccessible to their limited perceptions, thoughts, and senses. In this dimension, limitations and boundaries cease to exist and differences in race, ethnicity, culture, and gender are insignificant. Instead, the true value of each individual, which is the common essence among all human beings, governs" (*Theory "I"*).

Just like the fetus in a mother's womb, no one had to think about how to feed and raise the fetus. It was one with its own essence, which was full of knowledge and information for it to grow without any interruption. The same essential knowledge and motivation still exists within us, under the many layers of insignificant dust of information.

Prof. Nader Angha says, "This dimension remains buried under the multiple layers of misteaching and limitations imposed by social norms

     DR. ROHAM GHASSEMI

and habits. It is not nourished and developed and has no manifestation. Therefore, when human beings encounter the concept of spirituality, they tend to deny its existence. The artificial distance between the *i* and the *I*, between physical and spiritual dimensions, remains intact. As a result, human beings lose touch with reality in its unified form due to boundaries imposed on body and mind. To establish lost harmony, to get back in touch with reality, human beings have only one choice: to return to their original source of life, to the *I*, the point where being manifests itself in the form of matter" (*Theory "I"*).

If we realize the value of becoming closer to our inner self, to our *I*, we first need to take small steps toward changing our routine behavior and habits. Then we may be able to get rid of some of the limitations and boundaries that is taking us away from ourselves. We can call it the introduction to purification. Then my cognitive system will have some open space to learn about newfound knowledge.

Kurt Lewin says, "The repetition of an activity brings change both in the cognitive structure and in the need-tension systems. That's why when you know what you need, what you truly want internally, which is something that is not caused by comparison, judgment, greed, or jealousy, that is your true drive, that is an inner drive like thirst or hunger. The only way to satisfy that is to find water or food, so the inner drive just pushes you forward and you keep on searching and digging and wanting, the repetition will get you there."

Now let us see what things can obstruct our way to motivation for living healthy, so we can better recognize and avoid them.

1. Lack of Knowledge and Understanding

The amount of knowledge one possesses about any issue that one encounters is a key in determining whether or not they will succeed; for instance, having or lacking adequate knowledge about gardening will determine if you can or cannot plant and grow flowers in a pot or in your garden. Having beautiful flowers at home is one thing that seldom would anyone feel unhappy about, yet most tend to avoid buying and keeping them. Even if one's friends suggest that one should buy some plants and flowers to decorate one's home so they can enjoy it and to make their place a happier place, one may shrug it off, saying there is no time, no need, no energy, and, in other words, no motivation.

Now if we take a closer look, we would understand that this lack of motivation is first fueled by a lack of knowledge about keeping plants at home, and secondly by being unaware of the many benefits of keeping plants for one's mental health. Therefore, the individual may be able to convince oneself that there is no such need for the plant at all through different excuses. To be motivated to live healthy, one must be aware of the self-benefits and consequences of being motivated. Without this knowledge, one will use excuses to stop acting and moving forward and eventually replace the desire to move with a tendency to do nothing (laziness) and will come to call oneself as unmotivated. One has ignorantly convinced oneself of being unmotivated, which also applies for reasons for exercising, productivity, studying, and progress in general.

2. Lack of Role Models
   One of the biggest reasons that attracts individuals' interest toward something and motivates them to master a skill is having

a role model. As an example, an active, energetic father who exercises every day and goes hiking on weekends can be a role model and motivate the children to exercise. A lazy father who lies on the couch all day, smokes, and watches TV can become a role model of being unenergetic and lazy for his children. Therefore, those surrounding an individual and their function as role models have a direct link to one's mental and behavior patterns.

Let us suppose that the child of this lazy father meets an active and athletic coach, teacher, or instructor who does a lot of mountain climbing. What effects will this have on the child?

At first, the child will discover new ways to spend their leisure time, for example, by hiking or mountain climbing. Secondly, they will realize that they can integrate this mountain climbing habit into their own lives as well. Finally, they will come to understand why the teacher is so energetic and lively and why their own father is the opposite.

So having role models will always show new and different paths and approaches in doing things and living. In other words, it will reveal new possibilities and choices by broadening one's horizon, which helps one take the best options. Every individual can choose the best in any field as their role model, be it Einstein or Hawking in physics, Ronaldo in football, or Beethoven in music.

3. Comparison
   Superficial and shallow comparison of oneself with others is a harmful habit that can find its way into the lives of different

individuals of different age groups, especially when one has no concrete path and method to put one's efforts into and make one's life better. In such a situation, one is constantly concerned with other people's lives and their successes or failures, being oblivious to the fact that different individuals are blessed with different sets of talents and strengths.

More than often, one may see people of the same family have completely different talents; yet some parents, and out of pure ignorance, insist that their child should also pursue a degree in, say, medicine because that is what his or her cousin studied. If the child's potential and talents is elsewhere, this will not only end in disaster on an educational level, but also put a large gap between the individual and his true talent and also a gap between the parent and child, which may in turn develop into different mental disorders for either one or both of them.

Another example of unhealthy comparison is comparing one's own life with that of another. When young people compare their own lives and conditions with their peers and arrive at the conclusion that they are less fortunate than them, because they might have a better car, bigger room, more freedoms, and so on and so forth, such individuals bring upon themselves such a great disappointment and a weak morale, that it will leak into their family members' lives. For instance, they might call their parents losers and failures for having less money than their friends' parents, while those apparently prosperous families of their friends might not even be happier than their own and have many domestic problems themselves.

One must also take into consideration that a great many of world's successful people, such as scientists and politicians, have grown up in poor conditions as children and have suffered abuse, neglect, abandonment, lack of financial security, and so on; but they have found the strength and determination to be responsible for their own future and have raised above others to earn society's respect.

4. Judgment and Prejudice

This will require a lot of explanation, as one of the most problematic habits of thought that hinders motivation, desire, and a drive to move is judging and having prejudice. It seems that most individuals are blessed with an invisible knowledge that has the authority to judge different people and things before knowing anything about them. This kind of judgment is sometimes used on oneself and sometimes on others. Since this ancient habit is one that cannot be removed without proper upbringing and education and training, it is also one of the most common among people of different backgrounds and cultures, even when everyone is well aware of its dangers and faults. As with all other issues we encounter and one may face in life, this can almost never be helped until we discover it as a flaw and admit it exists.

We can simply see how judgment and prejudice can affect one's daily life, as one forces upon oneself the burden of judging and judgment, which is a subject that comes only with knowledge and wisdom. In other words, one will convince oneself of not needing real knowledge, and then they are constantly presuming to judge different matters and people.

There is no doubt that such judgment's undesirable consequences will firstly be suffered by the person that has judged, until they learn the unhealthy path that only leads to unhealthy results. It only takes one's mind away from their own self and ignoring all that one needs for self-awareness and actualization to be at peace.

CHAPTER FIVE

NOW THAT WE talked about motivation and knowledge, I am going to share a bit of information that may be useful. These are based on my trainings and research. I'm going to suggest some practices or exercises for individuals that would like to have more motivation during the day, week, or year. Some of you may already practice all or part of this list, so obviously, you can read and decide what is useful to you.

Diet and Nutrition

One of the most important things that one has to do throughout the day is to eat and nurture the body. No one can deny the huge role it plays in every area of one's life; therefore, you have to know what you are putting into your body and why. From the time we eat, all minerals get distributed in our body. Blood circulation, hormones, and neurons are but a few of the systems affected by what one eats.

Learning more about different types of food and one's physical needs is a necessary step in creating a balanced and healthy diet. Without such knowledge, one will have to take whatever they are served based on the eating habits of their country, culture, etc., without any choice. It is then necessary to know different ingredients and how to cook them so we can make healthier food choices.

One important problem among a lot of people is, they believe cooking and learning about food is a difficult and even unnecessary, and they will consequently eat whatever they are served without knowing if it is healthy or not. But especially now, with all the information on social media, it's as easy as spending fifteen minutes a day learning about them and fifteen minutes a day preparing the health meal.

Reading

Reading is perhaps one of the easiest and most basic things one can do regardless of their culture and level of education, but we often see that most people mistakenly see it as being too difficult, boring, unnecessary, and futile. It seems that it is a cultural trend to take every advice from social media and, apparently, love to gather information on tens of different subjects, but not the necessity basics, which helps in learning about actual sources of knowledge. Perhaps people believe that any book that they have read up to this moment in their lives is enough to make them such complete experts on everything in life, so they stop reading and learning. Some may think it would be meaningless to learn anymore, and thus are left alone with chaotic, hopeless thoughts, which are ironically the same thoughts that stop them from becoming motivated to live healthier, happier lives. Then they start to judge, as if I condemn myself not to live comfortably, not to go to sleep comfortably, and repeat the same pattern every day.

Making New Friends

Every one of us has a different mindset and image of relationships with others, from the simplest interpersonal interactions to deep intimate relationships. Some of us have a positive relationship with those who we come into contact with, while others do not possess this gift and have fewer connections and friends. One must note that we, by no means, want to imply that those with fewer friends are less healthy; what we would like to discuss are those barriers stopping us from creating more meaningful and constructive relationships throughout our lives.

Taking into account one's personality and interests, one can find friends to help make one's knowledge and world expand. Such friendships not only stop the parties from feeling unmotivated but also keep encouraging and driving them to move forward with their lives. So adding to one's knowledge itself can be a good motivator for making new friends with the same ideas about learning and growth, about peace and healthy living, even though one might initially judge it to be a pointless task.

Going to University or Taking Educational Courses

As influenced by one's immediate living environment—society—one might have a series of readily accepted beliefs about higher education in mind. For instance, the child of doctor whose uncle is also a doctor might find pursuing an advanced degree an easier and more necessary ingredient for success, in comparison with someone whose parents have not been to college and insist on more ordinary life and success rather than academic.

The complaints young people often come up with about education are mostly due to not having time and their being unaware of its great benefits. One of the most fundamental things one may learn at a university is being orderly and organized, whether it is on a mental level or an educational one, as in thinking and learning in time and questioning when it is due. After learning this skill students are educated and trained in their field of preference and will continue to make use of it. It is only after going to college or university with this mindset that one will grow fond of learning and understand the purpose of education.

A New Job

We have all met people who stay in a company or job that they despise for many years. It is as if they think this is all they deserve from life. Why do they keep on working like this? Is it something other than their own prejudgment? It can all be summarized into a fear of ifs. What if I cannot find another job and lose even what I have now? This fear condemns one to work months and years in a job one does not enjoy. One fears falling apart, even though one knows that change is an essential part of life and the process of growing.

Please note that we are not referring to a change without research, knowledge, or plan, but a change springing from taking into consideration one's future, professional growth, and inner satisfaction. If one would study and investigate thoroughly about a change in career instead of following a blind fear, one would be able to avoid the counsel of guesses and fear and make more constructive choices.

DR. ROHAM GHASSEMI

Workout Routines, Going to the Gym

Nowadays, going to the gym and regular exercising is one of the main characteristics of a successful energetic life. Considering its great biological, physiological, and mental effects on human beings, it can easily be regarded with the same level of importance as a healthy diet. The more one exercises with discipline and control, the more healthy and happily and full of energy one is able to pursue daily and long-term goals. As long as every movement and exercise is with full awareness that I'm focusing on myself, on my breathing, on my heartbeat, I focus to become aware of myself and therefore more energetic. I learn to do this for myself and how to preserve my energy for things that matter to my health.

As pointed out before, motivation is a keyword of our times, and it is discussed on different levels of our lives, be it social, educational, professional, or even matters such as financial management of one's life. It is not an uncommon belief that motivation is the force moving people to act toward achieving their personal goals without taking into consideration what other people's rights or feelings might deem necessary. Such selfish variation of motivation may only offer temporary and small benefits since selfishness and greed are undesirable and will eventually lead to disappointment. One needs to learn how to have a motivation that is both sustainable and able to bring us positive feedback and effects from and on our immediate surroundings.

Motivation has different forms and varieties for every individual, so it can be called personal motivation. This kind of motivation is, as the name suggests, about each person and all that is going on inside of them. It can only be discovered through giving oneself the chance to observe within and realize every individual has their own path to walk that is theirs and theirs alone. Until one has not discovered the importance of this uniqueness, one will lack motivation to walk and live one's path and life, and even if a path is found, without this knowledge, it is more likely a construct of others' motivation and ways of life, and will ultimately fail to answer one's own inner desires.

How to Practice and Maintain Motivation for Living Healthy

Before proceeding to begin the next part, I would like to ask the dear reader to take a look at the form below and try to briefly list their ideas and beliefs regarding their way of life, including, but not limited to, personal thoughts about your true self, one's true faith, things that impowers you, things that discourage you, things you like improve, how to deal with others, daily routines, etc. And if they follow no specific pattern or order and react to different events and peoples, they may write that as well.

The ways or rules of my everyday life:

1.

2.

3.

4.

5.

6.

7.

8.

9.

10.

11.

12.

.

First, it must be taken into account that each of us is responsible for our thoughts and lives. In other words, architects of the world we live in. Therefore, in accordance with one's current circumstances, one can control one's thoughts, desires, and expectations to feel terrible in the most ideal situation, or to be happy in the worst. Prof. Nader Angha says, "You are the creator of your environment."

The next few directions are to help influence our habits to create a better environment for myself.

1. Changing One's Habits and One's Comfort Zone
   Every individual is used to living life in a certain way learned or acquired through one's upbringing and cultural background. When one lives completely obedient to these and seldom presumes to think about changing some of the less beneficial ones, it is natural not to realize that some of such habits are actually roots of many different problems in one's life, such as fatigue, untidiness, lack of time, being unmotivated, boredom, etc. With little attention to one's sleeping patterns, diet, exercise plans (or lack of one!), and any and everything we do as our daily routines simply because we are used to, one will find ways to improve upon them and do these daily tasks in a way that will bring oneself, *I*, more satisfaction, happiness, and peace.

2. Not Rushing Things and Decisions
   Due to innumerable technological advancements of our age and the great speed at which tasks are done, decisions are made, and thoughts are thought, the ageless wisdom that one must think things through is being replaced by "I have to do it fast." A sound alternative is to take one single minute or more to think

                    DR. ROHAM GHASSEMI

important decisions through so one can better manage and plan one's daily life and make the best decisions

3. Being Organized

The more orderly the living environment under one's control is, the more control one feels over one's surroundings and, consequently, one's own thoughts and emotions. As we all are familiar with the opposite case, where one's thoughts and emotions slip out of one's grasp and into chaos because of a chaotic and disorganized living environment, this is a very helpful tool to help one make decisions firmly and to plan one's schedule with greater determination. We can think of it as a general rule that if one lives with discipline and a calculated order, one's thoughts and emotions may take more orderly forms, and thus, one's actions follow the same pattern. Once one is comfortable following such a system, one will have more confidence regarding one's plans and decisions more effectively.

4. Changing Daily Routines

Habits and living one's life, according to them, is one of the biggest obstacles to renewing one's life and to achieving new things. Therefore, one must not fear breaking some habits, and if one does so gradually and out of knowledge, it will lead to constructive changes and progress in one's life. Some people's daily lives have become so repetitively dull that they need not to even ask themselves why they do certain things in a certain way. For instance, staying awake all night without doing anything and sleeping half the day away.

Planning a new routine that is organized will undoubtedly mark a new beginning in one's life and it can be done over time to avoid disappointment.

5. Long- and Short-Term Goals

No climber has ever reached a summit without a goal. Just as accomplishing great things deems great goals necessary, maintaining such goals and not losing to obstacles requires smaller, short-term ones to keep one on the path and away from becoming disappointed. The resulting sense of satisfaction when completing these short-term goals gives one the required energy and encouragement to stay motivated and move toward the final aim. This means constant progress.

6. Helping Others and Being a Role Model

One of the most satisfying things to do for a healthy human being is to help other human beings. In some cultures, this principle is emphasized as an important personal duty since childhood, while in some others, it does not receive the same level of attention.

Since humans are social beings, they can influence their living environments just like they can be influenced by them. If one pays attention to this issue in one's daily life and tries to do everything with more control and awareness, one will soon realize such a great influence one can be on one's community and peers. On the other hand, if one introduces a certain level of chaos through control and awareness, it would still be possible to observe the effects on one's surroundings. So if one is constantly being influenced by one's surroundings and vice versa, why not influence others in the best and most constructive of ways to both help others and be a role model and also teach oneself responsibility of one's life?

7. Being Responsible for One's Own Actions
    Think of a morning as one wakes up and, according to the last night's sleep, is ready (or not so much) to start a new day. One starts the day either with control, order, and awareness, or with chaos and obliviousness. Last night's sleep still carries a weight on today's mental state and how one deals with the outside world as encountered throughout the day. The more one feels responsible for one's daily actions and sleep at night and also for one's thoughts and feelings, the more beneficial and sound will one's decisions be. On the contrary, if one deprives oneself of this truth and refuses to be responsible for controlling and organizing one's life, it would only be natural to lose order and blame others for all possible unpleasantness in one's life.

8. One's Social and Domestic Duties
    As pointed out before, humans are social beings and live in a community, such as a family. If we consider society to be created of families, it would mean that the family is a fundamental and basic unit that needs to fulfill its roles and function properly for both the society and itself to continue their existences in health and harmony. Individuals play the same role a family plays in the society. So long as individuals function properly and play their part, such as parent or child, the family will continue to live healthy and peacefully; the members will feel satisfied and contempt.

The problem arises when one or more member of the family refuses to do their part and leaves a gap in the system, and thus, the order and structure of the family crumbles down, and every member takes a different path. It is obvious that such a system has no option other than disintegration of its members.

Again, I would like to point out that great care has been taken to provide the reader with practical solutions and ways to become motivated. By contemplating and practicing to introduce these habits and points into one's life, the reader will, hopefully, enjoy the benefits.

I would like to ask the reader to introduce two of these concepts into their life, each two weeks in the next couple of months. You can write them in this table and keep track. It goes without mentioning that previous practices need to be continued as new ones are introduced.

Week 1

Week 2

Week 3

Week 4

Week 5

Week 6

Week 7

Week 8

          DR. ROHAM GHASSEMI

It must be taken into consideration that these new lifestyle choices may be quick and easy to implement for some, and slow and hard for others; therefore, you may shorten or lengthen the given time schedules and divide them into short- or long-term goals to match your personality and capacities so you can be aware of your progress.

Also consider that these practices need persistence, and you should not feel disappointed if you can only accomplish them for a short while or not at all. Do not lose heart, and keep trying until you achieve the desired results, no matter how many times it may fail or how long it may take.

INDEX

U

United States, 10

W

wisdom, 8, 12, 29
  inner, 12
    See also ideal self; real self